GEORGE SZIRTES

BAD MACHINE

BLOODAXE BOOKS

ISBN: 978 1 85224 957 1

First published in 2013 by
Bloodaxe Books Ltd,
Highgreen,
Tarset,
Northumberland NE48 1RP,

www.bloodaxebooks.com
For further information about Bloodaxe titles
please visit our website or write to
the above address for a catalogue.

Supported using public funding by
ARTS COUNCIL
ENGLAND

Cover design: Neil Astley & Pamela Robertson-Pearce.

Printed in Great Britain by
Bell & Bain Limited, Glasgow, Scotland.

CONTENTS

Magister

Grey Wood

Out of this wood do not desire to go. Here is where enchantment starts. Here is where confusion begins. Here rulers of different realms assume masks of faun, ass, wall, moon and lion.

Out of fallen beeches creep the ghosts of time. The wood is full of ghosts. Of burned leaves if nothing else. Then they disappear and then the trees are burned.

It is a strain talking on several levels like this. Wood is not wood. Ass is not ass. Wall is not wall. Enchantment is not enchantment. Talking like this is just talking. It is like being stripped naked.

The naked are enchanted. That is where we begin. That is a faun. That is a lion. The ghosts of time enter the wall. We don't talk of ghosts in walls. The wood is the ghost. The word is a ghost.

Here is where the confusion begins. It is a strain talking. Like this. Like that. What will they do with all that grey wood? Wood is not wood. Ass is not ass. It is like being stripped naked.

Colours

1

Burlywood, Chartreuse, Gainsboro, Ghostwhite, Greenberg,
Maroon, Orchid, Moccasin, Peru, Demosthenes, Snow,
Papayawhip, Popper, Peachpuff, Hotpink, Hothot,
Darkred, Darkgrey, Dodgerblue, Drudgery, Derrida,

Fuchsia, Fondle, Fricassee, Firebrick, Fenfall,
Coral, Cornsilk, Crimson, Coleridge, Coolidge, Honeydew,
Hellebore, Hartshorn, Honegger, Jet, Jellaby,
Lavenderblush, Lascar, Lightcyan, Lightlight,

Gray, Grey-Green, Garrulous, Golightly, Garrick,
Indignant, Insolence, Irked, Ivory, Ilk,
Jeremiad, Asclepius, Goldenrod, Arriviste, Glock,
Cyan, Chocolate, Cadetblue, Camisole,

Fallen Grey, Flecked, Lost Blue, Amaretto, Shrubbery,
Yearning, Absinthe, Abstinence, Grey Holes in Green.

2

Had these been voices, the wind might have sung them
Through a hedge or an empty head. It was winter
Then spring then summer then autumn. Thunder
And lightning. The beating of a red drum.

Had it been blue guitar, or purple rose, or black Sunday...
Had it been brown study, devil's dyke, or dun
As in dunnock... Had it been greyfriar or redeye
Or permanganate or potassium..

Had their names been their being... Had the retina
Been in service... Had the hot stores burned away
With the seasons... Had it been anything but dinner
In the provinces... Had the spectrum not gone awry...

Had it ever fallen out like this with the light lost
In the jungle of the voice with its brilliance and dust.

Dictionary
The problem of continuity – of syntax, to think of this is to think of something else

Ways of moving:
Pulse of wind, press of wind (as in fingers of wind gently pressing against eardrum), swandip, swanbulge, swanstretch, peeling (as in gull peeling, as in off the horizon, breaking into bribs and blebs,

Sound:
sussuration, sibilance, hissing, severance, slobbing, sisterance, haw, ha, hm, hrum, squak, squirk, settling, the sudden cry of a low-flying plane

Terrains:
sinking, mellifluous, aggregated, bled, sucking, defiant, drowned, eaten, desired, uncalled for, high and mighty, scrubby,
billowing with tesserae

Textures:
hair, skin, bullet, scraped, dinged,
screaming, phlegmatic,

buggered.

Densities:
breast,
haunch,
nape,
groin,
wire,
chain,
gravelled,
dreamt,
densest

Formations:
Fribbles and tangles, bouquets, knots,
serrations, military ranks, globules, bristlings,
efflorescence and inflorescence,

Clothing:

> hem, frill, armour plating, shipsteel, steelsheen, massed ranks of
> > stone jackets, yomping gear subtly coded,
> > > clots,
> > > > clegs

Auxiliary languages:

Driftwood letters from the destroyed alphabet, such as lower case f, i, j, c
(as if there might be a word, or series of words, a sentence perhaps under
the stones and boulders to be constructed.)

Homages: human offerings, (the deodands):
bright helpless bits of blunt blue,
startled yellow, intimated pink,
the fadings, deformations, ephemeralities,
evidences, beginnings of a palette.

Food: the floating egg,
zabaglione,
hundreds and thousands,
porridge,
soaked bread
grits,

Broader concepts to be dragged kicking and screaming into language:
the concept of a straight line of cloud pressing lightly down on its bed of language,
still working out its etymologies.

The Lump

You think of the universe and those lumps of rock
Hurtling through an incomprehensible space
And realise, not without a shock,
That one of them is your face.

Great lump that you are, parents drone in your sleep
As you lie lumpen in your childhood bed,
The lumps are falling through the deep
Chasms of your childish head.

Lumpen the day, night smoothes it with its dark,
The lumps begin to glow in their fixed scheme
Of being, each a leaping spark
Between dream and dream.

Great lump of a world, of word: a sugar cube
To sweeten emptiness with parts of speech.
Word shuffles down the syntax tube
Beyond all reach.

*

It is like laying stones out in a garden
according to some Zen pattern
whose rules are unwritten.

Stone after stone arranged around space
On an unpromising surface
But set into place

As if in possession of the secret
Of the universe, or at least the planet,
Like a voice saying *Not yet, not yet.*

Not yet and never, the pair a leitmotif
Endlessly recurring in relief:
Stone, grass, sand, leaf.

Postcard: From a Tower

1 *Tower*

Once I lived in a country of small disasters.
In cities of perpetual mourning, rain
fell black as creosote leaving a stain
we couldn't remove. Streets with whole clusters
of houses vanished. Towers, commercial signs,
doorways, post-boxes, churches, bungalows
barrelled in darkness; long, stabbing rows
of terrible showers. Even railway lines
were gone. I had been here before and lost
my bearings. Now they were lost again. Each small
disaster was a form of tenderness that cost
a life. It was tenderness that was falling through
the space between us. It was what we knew
that kept us here, that kept us alive at all.

2 *Reverse side*

What keeps us here, keeps us alive at all,
is tenderness of sorts, tight stabbing pains
we give familiar names to, that form chains
of association and enable us to call
out names: Desire, Anxiety, Distress
and Resignation... Names obliterate
whole streets. Someone arrives late
for a lost appointment. Someone makes a mess
looking for something. Someone's car arrives
at a locked door. All this is tenderness.
The rain comes down and nothing much survives.
You watch how people thread their way through acts
of being, through rooms and dreams and facts,
to arrive in dreams at this precise address.

Postcard: The Rower

1 *Rower*

At which point was the boat quite lost to sight?
At which point did the rower realise?
At which point did the single oar lose meaning?
At which point did the land entirely vanish?
At which point did the waves become a wall?
At which point did the mind become the sea?

Because if mind and wave and wall and sea
are of one substance, and the loss of sight
result in loss of meaning – so that wall
is where the mind is – should we realise
our utter loss, we might entirely vanish
into a sea that never had a meaning.

But then, being alone with lack of meaning,
blank sea and brittle oar, the place we vanish
into is somewhere we can't name as sea,
and where we drown is just an oversight.
There's nothing there to know or realise.
It's all the sound of wave hitting sea-wall.

I wish we could hear the voice that is the wall –
a single voice that concentrates all meaning
into oar or wave. How good to realise
that sense of being alone on a blank sea
in voice or name, to find ourselves in sight
of any land, even one due to vanish.

You'll find this card tomorrow. The days vanish
in the usual haze however we stonewall.
I like it here. The sea is quite a sight,
darker than usual, flat, yet still a sea.
The weeks are almost endless. I've been meaning
to write you this. A card, I realise

is just a gesture. One can't realise
all one's ambitions. I seem to vanish
in myself. I've long been out at sea
without a landmark, no familiar wall
to climb or peep over. What kind of meaning
could I ascribe to it? Where is the sight

equal to this? What wall holds meaning
the way this does? I realise the sea
is more than sight, and some things always vanish.

2 *Reverse side*

Received the parcel
Safely, many thanks, Bella[1].
Monday. Leamington[2].

Received the parcel
Safely. Now it is Wednesday
And the sea is calm.

Received the parcel
Safely in the second year
Of the war[3]. Thursday.

Received the parcel
Safely, with many thanks. Sea
Calm. Nellie, with love.

Received the parcel
Safely. It is still Friday
And the sea is calm.

[1] Name illegible. Bella or Ella or Nellie.

[2] Postcard sent from 30, Grove Street, Leamington Spa to Mrs W. Yerrill, 30,
Mount Road, Haverhill in Suffolk. Neither place is by the sea. The sea is inner.

[3] Postcard dated 16th September, 1915, a Tuesday.

Postcard: Joke Shop

1 *Joke Shop**

Do you remember the advertisements for Whoopee Cushions? Do you remember Jumping Beans? Do you remember Fart Powder, Itching Powder, Sneezing Powder? Do you remember powder? *Do you remember the Cockroach?* Blue Mouth? Exhaust Whistle? Disappearing Ink and Foaming Blood? *Do you remember blood?* Do you remember Fun Snaps, Detonators and Floating Eyeballs? Do you remember jokes? Do you remember the Rattle Snake Eggs? The Snake in a Mustard Tin? The Money Snatcher? The Squirt Ring? Do you remember Love Potion? Mystic Smoke and The Bloody Arm? *Have you had an armful? Do you remember the ambiguities as well as the explosions? Do you remember smells? Do you still have your eyes? Do you remember being exhausted? Do you remember your mouth?*

* http://www.onlinejokeshop.co.uk/practical_jokes/Others/

2 *Reverse side**

My darling when I finger your tiny bones and consider our fragility I cannot help wondering about our future. *hi sir, i want to learn about some little bombs for only to make man scared sound and little explosion and also have a timer. Sir i have been looking for these information for a long time, at the end i found your web page luckily it is important for this bomb to be homemade if there is a misunderstood part i'm sorry regards.* And I watch your eyes flicker, as mine too flicker. *Do you put want to put a hole in a concrete wall? Cutting through steel wall? Anti-personnel? Bring down an airplane in flight? Put a hole in an airport runway? Bring down a bridge or building (what type of bridge or building)? Taking out a car/truck/Hum-Vee/ tank? Do you just want to disable the car or do you want to ensure a kill of the occupants? Where are you located and what types of materials are available there?* Darling, I gently lick the stamp. I am delicate in my writing. My heart goes boom boom boom.

* http://www.boomershoot.org/general/BombHelp.htm#Littlebombs

From You to One

So there you were. Who
spoke then? Who noticed the blue
coat you wore? The light?

We were united
in our fury and had closed
the door when they knocked.

Theirs was not to do
or to die. They stood around
anxious, in a group.

What should one do now?
It was not something one was
used to. Sheer nightmare!

MINIMENTA
Postcards to Anselm Kiefer

1 Rubble, Light and Voice

1

Concrete and rubble: the Word
Produces its monuments.
Monstrous overheard
Conversations. Lost tenements.
Attics open to the elements.

2

We were leaving the wreckage.
Soon it was dark and the queue
Lengthened into a sleepless dream
We had somehow to live through
And, finally, to redeem
As if night itself were the passage.

3

A lost glove hanging on a fence,
A shoe without laces by the roadside,
The hand's abstraction, the foot's absence:

Marriage of invisible inconvenience.
Bridegroom stripped bare by the Bride.
Lost glove. Lost fence.

4

The rubble was the frightening thing.
So much had fallen and the rain
Was as much inside as outside.
Tiny pebbles were pretending to sing
To keep fear off. And then more rain
With nowhere to hide.

5

We were clerks of forgotten states.
We scribbled memos
That none of us would read,
Opened deals that would not close,
Followed leaders who could not lead.
We traded our empire for a single bead
Of light that broke us like cracked dinner plates.

6

The evening, shrimp-coloured and cool:
A late mild header into winter.
Soon enough dark morning, soon
Enough the splinter
Of ice stuck in the window, the moon
Stuck fast in the deserted lido, the pool
Blossoming into night,
Black as anthracite.

7

Sometimes you want to sing but as
You open your mouth the world shunts
Like a train and voice fails.
The failure is unimportant, hardly counts
In the scheme of things, but you're off the rails.
Sometimes voice is all a man has.

8

Under the rubble sleep the dead
Barely visible, as always.
You hardly want light there. Days
Collapse into visions. Night is preferable.
Light looks for trouble
Between broken limb and marble head.

9

A clear voice in the temple. The choir
Slowly focuses around her, holding her still
Like a glowing electric wire.
The charge travels through her and beyond.
The air is light and blond,
Sustained by oxygen, faintly surgical.

10

Layer upon layer of brick and cement.
In the park over the road trees blend
With evening. People cross
Roads, move along the pavement
With a certain pathos
Towards the day's end.

Postcard: Untitled, *monument*

1 *Untitled*, monument

Look, they have collapsed. The monuments
      have fallen one after the other. Mud
   covers them; guts and grit and blood,
so they're no longer granite but tents
blown inside out, fixed to a feeble stem.
      There's no more life in them.

They are as the world is, large and rough to the touch,
      hollow, yet full of air and the lost soul
   of whatever created them when it was in control
of itself and its fate. They did not stand for much,
but stood, as now they simply lie,
      without ever having taken a formal goodbye.

Imagine the body swollen, covered with tiny hairs
      that attract all the flying waste
   of the world, the body awkwardly placed
and disposed among rubble, tables and chairs,
left on a tip. The body weakly surrendered
      to the elements, never to be mended.

Body in ditch. Body on grass verge. Body curled
      around some loved thing. Body cracked
   wide open. Body stiff limbed, broken backed.
Body returning itself to the general world.
Body simply aged. Body shocked
      into trauma, permanently blocked.

There's something careless about all this, something
      incompetent and botched. If we lack grace
   it might be because we've never known our place
among the elements. Our words do not wing
their way home but hover in the air,
      between haplessness and despair.

So when monuments collapse, we're not surprised.
        The sadness doesn't last long,
    just long enough to improvise a song
or murmur a prayer, something human-sized,
quite the wrong-scale for a monument
            erected for at an all-too-large event.

2 *Reverse Side*

There was no wind, not any movement in the park where they were gathered. It was well beyond the edges of town, requiring a bus ride and even then some walking. They'd been arranged as if at a party, like guests trapped in a place they hadn't chosen to come to, but were obliged by others to attend because they were no longer welcome to occupy the spaces they had considered their own. Did they have anything in common that they could share? That had, of course, been the principle of their gathering, one that they themselves understood. 'So you're here too?' 'Do you remember…?' I can still sing the first three verses of…' 'Such things are, perhaps, inevitable, and yet…' And so they chattered on in their obscurity, for lack of drinks and other refreshment. One noted a certain tickling sensation at his ankles where the weeds had grown unmanageable. Another was pointing away from the sunrise but not quite at the sunset with unquenched ardency. The passions in their breasts were melancholy but still passions. 'We are returning to nature,' said one, 'if these weeds are anything to go by.' 'And nature regenerates,' another responded. The insects in the grass were singing *The Red Flag*. A bird whistled a bar from something they recognised as a *chastushka*. Still no wind. Still nothing stirring. 'Is time irredeemable?' asked one, sighing. 'We shall see,' another replied. 'Too early to tell,' added a third. The sun was moving their shadows, spreading them out on the grass which was growing and had never stopped growing. 'We must hurry,' said one. 'We cannot let the grass grow under our feet.' A small wind sprang up. 'Now we'll be all right,' they said. 'Now   at   last   we   can   breathe.'

The Best of All Possible Worlds

The best of all possible worlds is asleep
having turned in for the night.
It is dreaming of snow a mile deep.

The best of all possible worlds contemplates
its own reflection in the mirror,
its eyes two enormous plates.

The best of all possible worlds is at the bus stop
in a steady shower of rain
watching water fall, drop by drop.

The best of all possible worlds is tired
of waiting for the promised improvements.
It has run out of things to be desired.

The best of all possible worlds becomes
a nervous, clumsy abstraction
all fingers and thumbs.

The best of all possible worlds is a dark star
in a universe of its own making,
muttering: things are fine as they are.

Things are fine as they are, says the sun on the wall
Things are fine as they are, says the cold in the bones
Things are fine as they are in the best of all possible worlds.

Honour and Pride

The words honour and pride were used in abundance

Honour

We woke to find ourselves in the land of Honour,
The maps were bold but hardly accurate.
The capital kept shifting and the trains
Did not run on time.

We needed a Leader to make it happen.
We needed a Leader to show us where Honour lay.
We needed the back streets, the alleys, the sewers
Of Honour to be clean and presentable.

And yet we were always aware of the nature
And psychic geography of each of its cities.
We lived them and walked them, we caught
Its night buses, hailing its taxis.

Beyond the borders of Honour is wilderness.
Beyond the borders of Honour the creatures
Don't know their place in the Peaceable Kingdom,
Nor do we know it, we who inhabit it.

I woke myself dreaming of Honour, the Peaceable
Kingdom, speaking its language, its impeccable
Grammar, perfectly formed in the cavern of my mouth,
The attic of my brain, the cellars of my gut.

So Honour was mine, and the maps were redundant.
So Honour was spoken throughout the Peaceable Kingdom.
So Honour the omphalos, the lodestone, the centre.
So Honour that most honourable estate

Where nothing runs on time but the burnings proceed
Every evening, in our habitations, our tunnels,
In all the beautiful corpses of creatures,
In the words of my mouth.

Pride

The watch ticking
The back straightening
The shoulder broadening
The head rising clear of the neck.

The hand waving
The crowd proceeding
The birds in the square scattering
The heart filling the spaces prepared for it.

The soil parting
The first shoots extending
The tree that is forever to be growing
The leaves thrust together in the wind through the branches

Abstraction

From starting points, through abstraction, to control
is a process that demands a starting point
or else there is little point in starting.

So we begin by starting at a point that lends itself
to abstraction as a well-conducted process
and in that way we seek to take control.

Taking control is the point. That is the process
implied by abstraction, why it is worth starting.
Process is point. Alternatives are pointless.

This, then, is process, the point at which we started,
the reason we abstract the point. It's abstract,
an abstract point in the process of control.

There's no point in control, unless we take it
as the final point of a process of abstraction,
a point acknowledged at the very start.

And that is where we came in, at the start,
the point at which abstraction truly started,
and so it is that we are in control.

The English Vowels

after Rimbaud

A- Butter yellow, E- Ice blue, I – scarlet:
there's your beginning. So you move beyond,
to O – deep Brunswick Green, U – violet.
The butter-yellow thickly spread, bright blond

on breakfast tables. Meanwhile, ice blue E
greets day with a frozen look, its cold eye
shifting past the newspapers and coffee,
though nothing can suppress the scarlet I

in its heart, a cry rounded to fire shape
moving across the O of Brunswick Green:
the shock of declaration, a mouth agape
with grass. Elsewhere the poor shuffle between,

park and home, from underground to dole queue,
under the violet gaze, from A to U.

The Immigrant at Port Selda

I got off at Port Selda and looked out for the harbour
but it was quiet, nothing smelled of the sea,
all I saw was a station by a well-kept arbour
with a notice pinned to a tree.

It said: *Welcome to Port Selda, you who will never be*
our collective unconscious nor of our race.
This is the one true genealogical tree
and this the notice you will not deface.

It was beautiful there. It was Friday in late
autumn and all the birds of the county sang
their hearts out. I noted down the date.
The sun was shining and the church-bells rang.

Trojan Horse

London, thou art the flour of cities all
WILLIAM DUNBAR

New Troy cried Dunbar and so it was we entered
as if by stealth, wandering the suburbs
of her good pleasure, disorientated,
less an invading army than dizzy tourists
of our own helplessness, decentred,
tending to trip and stumble over kerbs,
our childish hands curled into childish fists,
our very strangeness oddly understated.

By the railway cuttings at Hendon we sat down
and thought how to weep when we remembered Zion,
but quite what Zion was we had forgotten.
The air we breathed contained a trace of it.
There was in the soil a particular shade of brown
that brought it back. Meanwhile the British lion
roared in the cinema so we should profit
from its power though the seats smelled rotten.

We stood in Trafalgar Square completely covered
in pigeons but looking all too pleased to find
such wholehearted acceptance. We were the boys
of the awkward squad, growing at an angle.
Occasionally perhaps one of us shivered
in the sheer tide of her, in the vast mind
of street-maps it took an alien to untangle,
as if she were not one but several Troys.

And sometimes now I see us as we were,
transported to the present, trying to keep warm
inside, selling *Big Issues* to ourselves,
sleeping in doorways even when in bed,
the street maps we know dissolving in a blur.
We're standing on an underground platform.
We're under Troy, tunnelling through her head,
riding without tickets, running with the wolves.

Meeting Walt, 1959

The year of Cuba and Sleeping Beauty, it was
my third year to heaven in a London Primary
with Mrs Haynes on dinner rounds, her summary
justice a smack with the spoon, reminding us
of virtue and the starving multitudes.
Dry pastry, streaks of grease, and scalding tea
in plastic cups – the cost of living in the free
world and cheap at the price. My father chewed
raw steak, my mother swam in garlic. Time
was lost in yellow smog, public monuments
still blackening in post-industrial grime.
We were the Empire and the map was ours.
We'd left behind our native tenements
For Walt, and Fidel, at home with the Great Powers.

At Rosehill Theatre, Whitehaven

(for Tony Roberts)

1

When Sir Nicholas opened the parachute
it was all silk stocking and cigarette holder,
the gruff dark of the bay was mute
and the mines stopped working for one microsecond.
The sea held its anger, a degree or so colder
as the invisible airmen drifted between peaks
where the deepest of deep lakes beckoned
the darkness to enter.

                         Sir Nicholas, genial,
eccentric, charming, speaks
with a foreign accent to the world beyond
the wilds of Cumberland and across the Atlantic pond.
He summons and plans and smokes,
organises, invites, speculates,
is amusing and congenial.
Sir Nicholas with his silken touch and the important matter
of the barn that is to become a theatre,
a small but glorious imperial vessel,
with the help of his friend, designer Oliver Messel.

Oliver Messel, genius of romantic flimflam
(*the flim flam floogie with the floyfloy*, cf. Calloway,
with a certain similar haunted love of play),
Messel, all gaiety and mask,
insists that whatsoever glitters must learn first to be sham.

2

Sham is the time, post-Eden and post-Suez,
Vicky and Osbert and Supermac
so *pure-Picasso*, darling, so pre-pop,
so dancing in Chelsea to trad or be-bop.
so *Who are the New Elizabethans?* so *Who is minding the shop?*

It is too late to go back.
It is the time of *as-new* and *as-new-as*.
It is in between. It doesn't know where to go.

But Sir Nicholas offers hospitality and art,
and the international cast duly appear
as the theatre, like a small red heart,
opens to all who can pay a quid or so
and don't think three bob a programme far too dear.

3

Hospitality and art. Someone has to pay
the piper and the virtuoso.
Here's where the rich come in useful.
You can't rely on some boho bozo
who has no contacts and doesn't have the pull
to make the great appear from far away.

So parachute in the maestro. Conviviality lends wings.
So Oistrakh plays the violin, Baker sings,
Gielgud recites, Joyce Grenfell monologues.
It's Miki's hospitality. The house entices
(the higher the art, the higher rise the prices).
You'll entertain and charm or quietly go to the dogs.

It's vision, darling, and who is to gainsay
the genuine Menuhin, Emlyn Williams, Annie Fisher?
You think I'm dropping names? Well, a gentleman may
occasionally be forgiven
for doing what all salesmen understand.
Music is music for any poor perisher.

And see! the perishers of Whitehaven
watching the arrival of the grand!

4

Shall we be breezy about all this or avoid the curse
of what is commonly referred to as light verse?
Oh no, breeze on, let each gesture be as light
as Seker silk, a soufflé on concert night!

Fook him, says the miner two miles out at sea.
What's Seker's silk or Messel's masque to me?

5

But Miki becomes president of am–dram and extends
the invitation to the townsfolk of Whitehaven,
(his employees after all, or some of them must be).
An entirely new audience, he says. New friends
and new blood. *A democratic institution.*
It is the perfect New Year Resolution
to drop the big S from society.

But Society and Culture are close allied in the mansions of heaven
much as they are on earth. So art flows on:
the hospitality, the stellar names, Peter Pears, Benjamin Luxon,
Brendel, Lupu, Gilels, with dancing to the Temperance Seven.

6

Hungarian stories tell of the marvellous palace spinning
for ever on a single duck's-foot base.
Illyés, the poet took it to make a satirical figure
with rich and poor in contrast. Now the grinning
prince presents us with his superabundant face.
May the palace be ever more splendid, ever bigger.

Look at this tiny theatre. Look at its scarlet plush.
Examine the silk that lines its heart.
Is that what hearts are lined with? What of the sow's ear?
The heart is music forever torn apart:
the silk purse rent, the coins that disappear
down a crevice. Genius Messel given the bum's rush.

Music has to congregate somewhere.
At the back of the pub, in a hedgerow, in the galley,
in the place of execution, down the lost alley
between two estates, even here, where its ghost
hangs in the throat, filling the lungs with air,
still beaming at its effervescent host,
still spinning, still winning.

7

You can take the boy out of the glamour, but you can't
take glamour out of the boy. Glamour and theatre.
Glamour and genius. Glamour and depth of feeling.
Glamour and generosity. Glamour and cant.
Glamour as something indubitably better.
Glamour as *putti* flying across a ceiling.

Fook that, repeats the underground man.

8

Maecenas is a silk mill, an address in Budapest,
let us say, *Rózsadomb*, the hill of roses,
an exclusive villa in an exclusive district.
Maecenas is Miki Seker. Music runs beneath us,
under both velvet waistcoat and string vest.
It continues long after the curtain closes,
Long after the last metronome has ticked.

9

So kind. Oh, so very kind. So delicious that accent.
So much missed. So much vanished.
Fook that. Fook that. Fook that.

It is never precisely what is meant
that kills us. It is love of what vanishes.

Time, Miki. Time's up.
Time to vanish. Pick up your silk top hat.

The music goes on. The perisher perishes.

Snapshots from a Riot

1

13 packets of fruit gums, 21 Yorkie bars:
this was the spree and all around the loot.
Below, the street, up there the sparkling stars
among the broken glass and burning cars,
the spree too small, a week's supply the loot,
13 packets of fruit gums, 21 Yorkie bars.

2

The good samaritans arrived, they helped him up
and took most tender care,
once he was walking, to open up his bag
and share the spoils, or what there was to share.

3

Sheneka Leigh, aged twenty-two,
was simply trying on a shoe,
footwear her besetting sin:
this is the box they threw her in.

4

He was peripheral,
a dot at the rim of vision,
with a stolen bottle of wine
a twelve year old before the district judge.
He'd *punched some 1 in the chest 2 times.*
Now see him move back to the periphery.
You watch your fucking face, his mother cries.
You watch your fucking face.

5

Brought up in circumstances more humble than they,
the righteous proclaim their humility.
The looters consider then pass on their way;
an exercise in futility.

The fatter, the fitter, the fleeter, the flitter
all of them suitably humble
as buildings and businesses crumble,
delighted and crowing and ever more bitter.

6

Payback time for not being taken on
by the job no one wanted but you.
So payback is paid
with both parties through.

7

CCTV is on the case. Watch the figures emerge
from the wallpaper then merge back in again.
Caught. Caught. And the commentary that chimes in:
Scum! Feral rats!
It is as well to distinguish them from the domestic sort
who are not about to flee the ship.

8

Zero Tolerance on Ground Zero:
the proper platform for a proper hero.
The toiling masses gather in the Forum
without ever quite forming a quorum.

9

A boy holds up a pair of jeans appraisingly.
It goes with the hood and the mask.
It is an aesthetic matter.

Children of Albion

Children of Albion, the future is yours,
It's safe now to wander and gambol outdoors,
The streets are all empty, the shops are all bare,
There's nothing to take but a breath of fresh air,
Nothing is broken that time won't repair
Children of Albion
Sleep easy

Children of Albion, the future is bright,
There's plenty of fire to light up the night,
The goods are all free, the watches, the shoes,
The TVs, the iPhones, the music, the booze,
There's plenty to gain when there's nothing to lose,
Children of Albion
Sleep easy.

Children of Albion, your life is your own,
You've nothing to do with the lives you have blown,
You can blame it on God, the Tories, the state,
On parents, on culture, on school or your mate,
On coppers, on joblessness, weather, and fate,
Children of Albion
Sleep easy

Children of Albion, you can take off that hood,
The world is your oyster, you're out of the wood,
Directors and bankers have run off with more,
They've been there before you, they've cleaned out the store,
They've lit their own fires on the trading room floor,
Children of Albion
Sleep easy.

Children of Albion, sleep well in your beds,
There's nothing to fear, no price on your heads,
No price and no buyer, you've romped and you've played
And there in your hands is the loot you can trade,
Let none be deceived, let none be afraid,
Children of Albion
Sleep easy.

Goroo

'Oh, my lungs and liver, what do you want? Oh, goroo, goroo!'

I was so much dismayed by these words, and particularly by the repetition of the last unknown one, which was a kind of rattle in his throat, that I could make no answer. [...]

'Oh – goroo! – how much for the jacket?'

'Half-a-crown,' I answered, recovering myself.

'Oh, my lungs and liver,' cried the old man, 'no! Oh, my eyes, no! Oh, my limbs, no! Eighteenpence. Goroo!'

Every time he uttered this ejaculation, his eyes seemed to be in danger of starting out...

David Copperfield

1

I have myself uttered such sounds as *goroo* when
the phlegm rose in me and my savage indignation
blew me purple. My lungs and liver were of no use,
nor my eyes that did verily start from their sockets.
Believe me, sir, it was no borborygmus but my fury.

So let me wind myself round my fit and fury
because what rises from the gorge or the sockets
of the eyes is a creature seeking to be of use,
and I have occasions, I assure you, for indignation
that cometh upon me, sir, just as and when.

2

It is injustice, sir, that lodges in my gut,
that and cheap jackets, cheap suits and all things cheap –
and we spit up cheapness, sir indeed we do
and eyes and limbs are as nothing in the action,
are as foul fog in the lung or failure of liver.

What after all would you give me for these lungs, this liver?
What is the injustice that is a call to action?
Good Lord sir, we spit it up as we must and do.
And life is phlegm and savage, and this is a cheap
jacket, and, causes the deep *goroo* that rises from the gut.

3

And so it is eyes start from their sockets. Enough
the eye, or a pair of lungs. *Goroo goroo*
is a clearing of the throat which is connected
to the viscera in my kind. You'll know my kind
as you proceed on your way down the street.

I have the habitation of the street.
I take no delight, sir, in the kindness of the kind.
Eighteen pence and my gut are, I assure you, connected.
My rates of exchange are *goroo, goroo* and *goroo.*
Here is your jacket. Here's mine. Is that enough?

The Cat Speaks of Hunger

I have made my peace with hunger.
It's a flea behind my ear. I scratch it
on demand. I am all soft landings,
quizzical windings, but hunger
is what winds in me. I watch it,
sharp as that beam of light stuck
fast in the glass. It seems to point
to a speck I must capture, toy with,
and consume. So it consumes me.
My nerves radiate from it, a coil of want
that curls me up when it settles.

Hunger is the missing, the desolate
part of me. I own it as I own my calm.
I pad around on it. I scratch myself.
I roll around in the beam of sharp light.
Hunger arches my back. I hang my coat on it.

Postcard: Thirty-three Propositions

1 *Thirty-three Propositions*

A number is a form of proposition
Syntax is a setting forth of numbers
Propositions are limited in number

Say, your life, has a span of limited numbers
That number too is a form of proposition
Say, we start here with this proposition

Let us make this our primary proposition
Let us propose a god of limited numbers
So we begin at a number more than number

A birthdate, or address, or telephone number
That proposes what might act as proposition
And, say, we call this, the good proposition

We like its syntax, accept the proposition,
And enter upon life with this bare number
The number meaning us, that is our number

Our proposition placed in terms of number
Say, a tattoo, a form, a proposition
We have to regard as more than proposition

A perfect-syntax, murderous proposition
That simply tells us that it has our number
And that our number is up, no more a number

Meaning we ourselves are a lost number
The syntax of our bones its proposition
Our atoms, cells and bones all proposition

Because this happens. Such a proposition
Is often made to those without a number
As also to those who might become a number

Here is the form: you just enter your number
That is a pretty simple proposition
Simplicity itself is proposition

Say simply this then: here's the proposition
You sign your name, and you become the number
They're in the form, in numbers beyond number

2 *Reverse side: Thirty-three Propositional Stories*

The little boy who escaped from the house became a serpent.
The little boy entered the house of the witches and sat there transfixed.
The little boy was a guest at the feast of the pudding.

Meanwhile back in the house, the pots were boiling.
Meanwhile the witches spoke the word of power.
Meanwhile the peasants jostled at the wedding.

Came there a maiden in the brilliance of her garments.
Came there the raven in his black tie and cape.
Came there the bridegroom with his retinue.

Nothing disturbed the long night of the suitors.
Nothing disturbed the scattering of the guests.
Nothing disturbed the cook in his reverie.

The light streamed in through the carriage window.
The light was a gift of the imperious godhead.
The light ran wild in the forest as if in pure panic.

It was not the intervention for which they had prayed.
It was not the end of the day, nor quite the morning.
It was not altogether clear where they were to meet.

The messengers declared the nature of their mission.
The messengers wore gold braid and frogging.
The messengers were summarily executed.

Soon it was winter and the trees bent in sorrow.
Soon it was winter and the abbey was deserted.
Soon it was winter: a time of fire and gifts.

Their dreams were disastrous, things were collapsing.
Their dreams were not be trusted. Their dreams could betray them.
Their dreams were the last haunt of witches and weddings.

Sounded the trumpet. They woke. It was morning.
Sounded the trumpet. The cockerel was dancing.
Sounded the trumpet in the far distance, or so they thought.

The little boy was a full grown man at last.
The little boy had come into his estate.
The little boy told the story of his becoming.

Dreaming the Budapest Zoo

1

Coming home late at night I met a fox
in the drive scavenging from bins.
He found an abandoned cardboard box
containing remnants of old curtains

and dragged it along. A cat yowled. The hedge
rustled. Windows blinked and glared
above us both. It was what we shared
of the moment, that and the narrow passage

the fox was just sneaking through
between two dark houses, as I was sneaking
through my various lives, with my own crew

of *doppelgängers* and familiars, my speaking
likenesses, creatures that ran or flew
beyond me or groaned like ice breaking.

2

The zoo was *Art Nouveau*, art's version of nature,
but I had never liked nature, and would choose
art every time. I preferred the human signature
to God's or the world's. I liked the blues

as people sing it, lamenting the human act,
the cussedness of circumstance. The dead
were my history, not trees, the artefact
not the fact it purported to embed.

I saw with my own eyes what the mind
could accommodate and longed
to accommodate it. I had designed

the arbours where my personal creatures thronged,
each in its corruption, each after its kind,
so every single bestial thing *belonged*.

3

Some unspoken, undigested, half-dream
is running under broken soil. The gorge
rises. Creatures freak out. The stars gleam
with an extra fierceness: their light seems to surge

through us. Suddenly we are luminous and feral,
as we've always been and know it. I struggle
to name the animals but cannot grasp their ephemeral
essence. However I call them, they wriggle

and bite and scratch. I am hardly myself. My eyes
have turned inwards to face the moon within. The stars
have nothing intelligible to say, emitting howls and cries

beyond interpretation. Between the cars
the thunder of worlds stampeding, the buzz of flies,
the burning carcasses behind the bars.

Fish Music

(for Pascale Petit)

He struggles into his borrowed human skin,
the one he wears for special occasions
with the sewn-in dinner jacket and polished patent feet.
He brushes off earth and other traces of night,
Smells the remnant darkness on his sleeve,
Bends back the fingers that constitute his living,
And picks up the instrument. His mother is listening
In the next room, holding her breath for him,
The breath she has been saving all her adult years.

After the skin, the fish scales. One must glitter.
One must swim through the day. He flicks his tail
This way and that. He makes the first sounds
Those scraped sighs that are the sign of his well-being.
'I'm ready,' he says, his eyes glassy and round.
'I've got my gills on. The whole amphibian kit.'

The music begins. The sea waits by the door.
Both skin and scale are glowing. The neck he wears
Is just a little loose, he must tighten it.
The chin has worn away on his left side.
The music slops about inside his belly a while
Then creeps upward blowing through his ears
Into the room and hard against the walls.
Now he is swimming. He sees the music
Floating in the tank of the room. He must practice harder.
It is his food after all. He can feel its strands
Slip between his fingers, now silk, now knife.
It smells wholesome, of water, night and skin.

'How does it sound?' he asks her. 'Like salt,' she says,
'Like salt and damascene.' Her fancy talk, he thinks.

It's not his skin, he knows that. The dinner jacket
Is of another era. Too many buttons on the waistcoat
Of the flesh. Too much blood in the fibre, none of it his.
But music too is skin. He wraps it about him.

He's hardly there: half-fish–half-man is elsewhere,
In the bone beneath a skin that's not his own.
Each living thing has its own element, he thinks,
And even this old skin belongs to someone.

Some Sayings about the Snake

after Helen Rousseau

The snake is imaginary, even in life.

We know it from a ribbon by its windings.

We know it by its movement, eyes, and fangs.

We know it from the apprehension we feel dreaming of it.

The snake arrives at dawn with the first light.

It enters through the ear and exits through the navel.

It coils itself within the gut and heart.

The snake is the primal scream in the grass.

It coils around the limbs of man and tree.

It lives under a stone in the guilty conscience.

It is necklace and armlet and bangle and song.

The snake is the air in a hollow tube.

The snake measures time the way man measures cloth.

The snake spells out its name in the sand.

The snake lives at the edges of life.

When the snake enters a book, the book closes.

Snake Ghost

after Helen Rousseau

There is nothing
  Quite so pale
    As the ghost of a snake
  In the lining
Of the oesophagus
  In a wisp of fog
    In the coils
  Of pencil shavings
And shorn hair.
  There is a word
    For the ghost
  Of the dead snake
That cannot be spoken
  That has vanished
    In the moment
  Of its conception
Which is less
  Than silence
    Than thinking
  Or waiting.

Postcard: The Swan's Reflection

after Caroline Wright

1 *Cygnus*

I am calligraphy. On salt marsh, on the village pond,
I write my name in arabesques. I speak white
To the cloud and the clouded water.
I am the furthest quarter
Of the starless night
And beyond.

I am breast
And wind and moon
And the sheer distance
Of constellations, the persistence
Of desire, the nebulae of systems soon
To vanish: cry and echo, curvature and rest.

2 *Reverse Side*

Call now.
The phone is on mute.
There is no speech, no language
Lodged in those empty spaces, no gauge
That can measure a distance so silent and absolute
We cannot address it in words, because we don't know how.

Listen to the street. The voices in shops, in the bus queue,
On the platform. Something curves back at us,
Some echo, arabesque, a kind of pageant,
Like the rhythms of an imagined
Language: *sign, Cygnus,*
Me, you.

Words from a Diary

Forgetting... once known, that first time...
Through curved ploughed field..., the opening up.
It was joyous, the crooked spire...
It was like taking words from a mouth or a rhyme
From coincidence on the chance
That the roulette wheel might stop
At the right place, given due circumstance,
At the very moment of desire,
With *all of you running amok in the empty rooms...*

What else to take from a mouth except a voice
saying *It was joyous*, that there were
No plates for the picnic and the rain, the storm...?
To seek in the word joyous an occasion to rejoice
As though imagination might seize
Whatever happiness there was on offer.
Catching delight is like catching a disease
And giving it a temporary form,
With *all of you running amok in the empty rooms...*

And *the fridge filled with dead animals*
And *the ceiling cracked* which is *the beginning*
Of an ending and *leaving Radio 4 on...*
This is the way each word falls
Into language and through it. And as for me...?
Black cherries, the orchard, a steep hill and our bodies spinning
Towards something I cannot quite see
In language, something lost, as if undone,
The mind *running amok* through all its *empty rooms*.

Half an Eye

Anyone with half an eye for dreams,
Night terrors, *idées fixes* or empty beds,
Anyone coming apart at the seams
Might do worse than imagine these vast heads
At conference or board. They might discern
Raw fingers and pink snouts, predator's teeth
In thin slit lips. Their eyes might learn
A new language, come at it from beneath
Paunches stuffed with human dross. *There is*
A figure full of promise, they might cry, seeing the future.
Can you make it out? Can you devise theories
Holistic, wholesome or unholy to ensure
Its grim existence? Let the terrible
Stay that way for ever. Let nightmares measure
Our lives. Leave them be. Steer clear of trouble.

Prospero

Prospero at his desk. Prospero
Entertaining visitors in his cave.
The libation of ghosts at feasts. Brave
Evenings of magical conversation. A glow
Redolent of winter moons with a grave
Star's dying fall. Veils. Shimmers. The officers
Courteous, the troops assembled in trenches
Under fire. *If you die, don't die by inches.*
Pistols at ready! Move forward! The dressers
Hoard bright secrets. A medal of words strung
About a shaman's neck. An island among
Merdes and talismans. A little *sturm und drang.*

Paleface

Americans get the best of the deal.
No longer colonials, they can be gentlemen
Twice removed. The cabbie at the wheel
Harangues the professor in the demotic *parole*
Of an overcrowded *langue*. All those sudden
Nightmarish dislocations of the soul.
You hardly know where to start. But then
Haply you meet a Lithuanian poet or
Exchange notes with a Venetian grandee.
Come to think of it, it is hard to see
How a European can fail to remember the unfor-
Tunate isles he has escaped from all too recently.

The Lost

Disused sheds might store a lot of garbage:
Elegies no longer wanted by the zeitgeist,
Republics of blood and gut, figures of Christ
Eviscerated by the press, some local carnage
Known of and reported, then forgotten.
Maybe eloquence is a matter of editing
And friendship. In any case, something
Hangs by these: the deaths, the rotten
Obits of a people bred on memory.
No slogan is ever free of flummery.

Southern Belle

Jerusalem, my happy home. Something judders
On the air, a special piece of darkness
Hidden in light. It is a hymn to tiredness,
Nightingale-ridden, haunted by ladders,
Counting its stars on a pale abacus.
Robin waits on his imperious aunt.
Over come the girls. Swans are floating
White dresses against dark blue. He can't
Escape the consequences of their flirting.
Red flows the blood. Red runs the water,
A terrible quiet settles
Neatly on its bed of molten metals.
Somewhere an old man woos the daughter
Of the house, whispering dryly in her
Maidenly ear while night hackles his fur.

MINIMENTA
Postcards to Anselm Kiefer

2 Wind, Cloud, Drilling

How often have we watched trees
move against dark cloud, their frail
armature part collapsed, part thrust
against the wind, the leaf-sail
of each bud billowing to squeeze
light from dark, energy from dust?

*

Unrest. The un-ness of things. Twig
like a broken *No*. Concrete steps.
A drill. A bulldozer. The cold lips
of November pursed for a kiss
that is more like a blow and all this
far too late, too troubled and too big.

*

Everywhere the human voice. How can
we help but hear it in grass and air?
Even a wall is only a tall noise with brick
syntax. High clouds whisper human
non-sequiturs that turn to rain. Where
can we hide? Why this sense of panic?

*

A man and woman in a field. The rain
starts and they take shelter. The grass
runs all one way. They embrace. They hold
each other as if they could not do so ever again.
Above them leaves fold and unfold
in the downpour that will quickly pass.

*

The construction site constructing.
The square empty but for machinery.
The cafeteria with its litter of trays.

Everywhere institutions. The lost days.
All this will be broken up, everything.
There will be no drama, only scenery.

*

And then he turned to her and ran
the back of his hand against her cheek
very lightly. It was as if wind had stroked any
surface whatsoever. He was an old man
or a young man, and she could not speak
or find words because there were too many.

Canzone: The Small of the Back

He who has numbered the hairs on your head and knows
precisely the finite number of blades of grass
in the open field and the grove full of flowers, knows
to perfection each little part of you. He knows
the elements, how they are composed, how small
and perishable they are and we are. He knows
our limits, our beginnings and endings, knows
days and minutes, counting them forward and back
and forward again as in dreams. There's no going back
for us, but for him it's the same either way. He knows
about forward and back, has counted the grass in the field
that stretches forever, a closed yet open field

in which numbers alone constitute the field.
And what do we constitute? The doctor knows
what lies within his own professional field.
I see his ginger hair, his black bag, the broad field
of his back as he crosses the street and over the grass
verge, up the drive with its gravel. His field
is comprehensible, part of a bigger field.
He copes and prescribes for a body of small
disasters, for a self that has shrunk to a small
map of the world. His numbers cover the field
entirely. I only know the small of your back
in my hands, the hour of night that will not come back

to greet us. I move to touch the small of your back
where it narrows before widening. My field
of operations is narrow. I stroke down your back
then up it again. It is ageless. As if time could look back
on itself while moving forward. The body knows
time as movement: as rise, crest, fall, then back
to where it started. So my hand knows your back.
It is marble and milk and summer and smooth grass.
We were stretched out together, lying on the grass.
It was summer in London. You lay on your back.
Below us the hill rolled away. The traffic was small
creases on a vast map, we ourselves distant and small.

He who has numbered the hairs on your head, the small
god we imagine moving through grass at the back
of our minds, counting the seconds, the god of small
comforts, of minutiae, of all the vast small-
ness of the universe that is this field and that field,
the god of the moment – that god knows the small
of your back better than I do. He comprehends the small.
We want him to number us, want someone who knows
what number is and means, someone who knows
the time, who binds us to a world that is always too small.
We want him to number all the blades of grass.
We ourselves want to lie out on that grass.

We know the words. We know all flesh is grass.
We're handfuls of dust, breathing in dust. Our small
numbers are divinities of dust and grass.
There's nothing better than dust and the fresh grass
on which you lie – I feel the small of your back
smooth under my hand, the field of grass
rolling away. Here is the image of grass.
The image of time lies somewhere in the field
where people are running beyond our visual field.
They are, like us, a movement in the grass.
They are familiar names that no one knows.
They are the moments everybody knows.

Grass is a cloud of green. The god who knows
each blade is counting them up. Beyond the field
lie houses and chairs and beds. Still further back:
the road down to the coast, the beach, the small
waves nudging over the scree, the dunes, the grass.

Footnotes

The last time I met my feet
They reminded me how rarely
We got to meet at all
So nakedly and barely.

The nails were hardly human
The toes were animal.
My contact with my soles
Was minimal.

It was a little like
Being an amnesiac,
I couldn't remember my face
Or recognise my back.

Somewhere in a morgue,
Raising a plastic sheet,
A lost-property clerk
Points out a pair of feet.

The feet are bare as life
And dead as a distant moon.
Dear feet, while you're my own
Let's meet again, and soon.

*

I remember my mother painting her toenails scarlet.
So little understood of the nature of becoming
While all the time becoming.

And later the tickling and the gripping of toes,
The shedding of the shoes.

*

From white sandals to sturdy shoes
The smack of the ball in the playground.
I grew slovenly and loutish as a boy,
All I could do was pound.

It was later the dancing came,
She taught me the steps and I trod
Lightly with precision,
Delicately shod.

*

He had a cupboard full of shoes
That had belonged to his late wife.
Since it was raining heavily
He offered you a pair,
Which you politely declined.

Was it superstition or genuine dread,
Not wanting to tread
The path of the dead,
Or just preferring to choose
Your own shoes?

*

It is the dancing we most love,
The shoes airborne as if we weighed less
Than we do, as if we might skip and soar
In everything we wore,
In our heavy human dress,
In that animal-skin glove,
In a phrase so perfectly put
That shoe becomes the foot.

Canzone: A Fantasy after Roethke

'I knew a woman lovely in her bones...'

...Ah, when she moved, she moved more ways than one,
But that's just movement as the cat performs,
Beauty enough for cats, for anyone
Because a movement can be more than one
And several is how they spent the day.
And she was several, far more than one,
Just more perhaps of one than anyone
In terms of movement, nothing standing still
For long enough, though they themselves stood still
While moving on, refusing just the one
Mode of movement or fixity of place
And so they kept on moving, place to place.

And this is where they were. This was the place
Where she was moving, every movement one
With the next, each fitting into place
Then shifting on; discarding sense of place.
And he stood by, seeing how grace performs
Itself, and knows its place beyond the place
Provided for it, never the perfect place.
You love the many and you love the one
But many may be focused into one.
You want the thing, you want it in a place.
You want it how you want it, to be still,
As poised, he thought, and constant as if still

In movement, loving all that remained still
In her, her sense of being in a place,
Not of it, and the sense he made was still
A point of stillness in her being still.
So when she moved it was more ways than one,
He noted, as she moved by being still.
One might move so and yet remain quite still
He said. It's life that holds her and performs
The daily ritual she herself performs,
And she performs herself beyond the one
Still moment of performance in the day
That moves past her and will not spare a day.

But this was where she moved, it being day
She moved through, as though perfectly at one
With day, and it with her, day after day,
With nights to come, the body of the day
Turning to sleep and image in the place
They lay and moved in, in a dream of day
Working its way through body and the day
As though her body, his dream, and day were one.
Most time is timeless. Time knows only one
Mode of being, rushing through the day
Ticking off items, the function it performs
Performable, but not what she performs.

They were, he thought, what permanence performs
When permanence is saved for just one day.
So day performs, so anything performs
Itself by moving, being what performs,
Because performance is like standing still
While moving. And so everything performs:
Movement, stillness, whatever thing performs
What happens. And it happens in this place
Or that, the whole being only the place
She moves in and, by moving in, performs.
So she, he thought, must clearly be the one
Who holds the movement still, as if at one

With both the stillness and the movement, one
Moment here or there, then the whole place.
Her body moved, and then she stopped quite still,
Still as the world compacted into day,
Her several parts, and all that day performs.

Actaeon

O, my America, my Newfoundland
JOHN DONNE, Elegy 20

O, my America, discovered by slim chance,
behind, as it seemed, a washing line
I shoved aside without thinking –
does desire have thoughts or define
its object, consuming all in a glance?

You, with your several flesh sinking
upon itself in attitudes of hurt,
while the dogs at my heels
growl at the strange red shirt
under a horned moon, you, drinking

night water – tell me what the eye steals
or borrows. What can't we let go
without protest? My own body turns
against me as I sense it grow
contrary. Whatever night reveals

is dangerously toothed. And so the body burns
as if torn by sheer profusion of skin
and cry. It wears its ragged dress
like something it once found comfort in,
the kind of comfort even a dog learns

by scent. So flesh falls away, ever less
human, like desire itself, though pain
still registers in the terrible balance
the mind seems so reluctant to retain,
o, my America, my nakedness!

Demi Monde

after Brassaï

It's where desire drives us, to this truce
In the sex wars where the dark fawns over
A plump thigh and fixed stare,
Where everyone is glad to be of use
Providing there is adequate cover
And smoke fills every cubic inch of air.

A woman is a man who is a woman:
Flesh parts itself in mirrors, turns around
To watch itself undress. Root and sap and urge
Move over cold sheets. There is no one
To talk to in the psychic underground
From which your face is waiting to emerge.

You cake yourself in paint, become the scent
That you've been trailing through passages
Of dreamless night. Flick through the address book.
Find your own name and prepare to experiment.
Flesh leaves behind its cryptic messages.
See, there you are, if you but care to look.

Nautilus

A quotation mark in space around the hollow
bones of the universe. A carousel spinning out of control.
You're flung off to the bottom of a scroll
of dark where nobody can follow.
These metaphors for all that is outside you –
the vortices of the scary-beautiful –
look, they are inside you. You feel the pull
of your own heart as the universe rides you.
Those yellow flowers in that earthenware jug.
The spill of wind under eaves. Where are we?
Where are our co-ordinates? A fly dances
on a skim of air. It's as if life were a drug
in the system. The universe spins free
of us. Here's where we are. Here's where we take our chances.

*

Chances, and several. The way sun dips across
a wall, the angle at which rain strikes a face.
Chance just has it so, that in one place
devastation, another the mourning of loss,
and here such happiness it fills a minute
for ever. I couldn't keep my eyes off the older
woman's face, as if I were its only beholder,
its sad crumpled beauty, its cabinet
of curiosities. I can scarcely believe my own.
Or yours, how the whole structure is maintained
and holds firm. Somehow we have gained
the world and are losing it in every bone
and cell, as if to chance. You eyes touch mine
in chance light, in perfection, as in rain.

*

Three times this week I have trodden on a shell
on the lower step when it was very dark
and I was too preoccupied to mark
the point at which it cracked before. The smell
of wet grass was gentle, intoxicating.
Clouds were bruises of thunder, the light mere spots
up ahead. Distinctions were lost in knots
of deeper or fainter black. My bed was waiting
for my mind to wind right down. Meanwhile at home
you lay in ours as if at the back of time
that too was waiting to draw and settle us
into its own bed. Like the snail in its brittle dome
it waited, and we rose next day to this rhyme
that swims out of the dark, this nautilus.

Plain: A Seventies Marriage

It was all very simple; plain brick walls that spoke
to the plain of speech; strict, suburban, decorous,
a little fierce, a little dull, with just a touch of malice
in their bones. But this July day broke

with sunlight creeping through its pores, the sky
blown clear to blue, luminous with the hours.
And there they stood among the elders in showers
of light, she in her veil, he in his bow-tie,

moving politely round the hall to thank the congregation,
family, friends, faces from the neighbourhood,
having tied the knot, to plain words, with plain food,
and then were quietly driven to the station

where the train took them away into new lives
into the years to follow: husbands, wives.

*

So the train took them, cruising through the dark
into the north and out to the hotel.
Nearby, the ferry waited on the swell
of the gale, a listing, lurching, drink-swilled ark,

while back in his room far off, the plain cross scratched
on exercise paper in ball-point pen was peeling away
as later their clothes would, leaving the light to pray
for itself, grow indistinct and untouched.

So forward and forward, and the plain bricks continued
plain, and the ministers changed, deacons came
and went, and the plain-faced God remained the same,
while the sea rose and dipped, strong, bladdered, sinewed,

wired with tides, all through July, and the clothes
lay where they dropped: high poetry, plain prose.

Canzone: Bad Machine

And so they handed me the bad machine
that seemed to me a miracle when new.
This, they said to me, was the machine
I'd have to play with now, this grave machine
whose workings were beyond me. It was mine
for ever, as long as any grave machine
could be, since it was only a machine,
albeit miraculous. And oh, the many parts
there were to it! I could move whole parts
and not even know that somehow the machine
was on. They'll care for it, I thought. If care
was what it needed *they* could give it care.

And yes I did, in subtle ways, quite care.
It was, after all, my very own machine,
and others at first also lavished care
on it. They bathed it, tucked it up, took care
it should be sound, kept it as good as new,
insisting, in turn, that I too should take care
with all they cared for, such parental care
being only natural. They called it mine
but it felt almost like theirs. I cried out: *Mine!*
It's mine alone, let go! They didn't care
what I thought then. They played their given parts
as I played mine. All had their private parts.

It is the younger party that departs
and so it was with me. I took some care
to make the parting easy. So one parts.
Parting is all we know of heaven. My parts
were working. I was the fit machine,
each chamber of my being full of parts
that wheezed and slid along with other parts.
The bad machine was good, as good as new.
I strode out and the world itself was new,
delightful, with discreet and lovely parts.
The way was open and the way was mine
to choose, or try at least to make choice mine.

71

Then everything was mine or beyond mine.
And parts were lovely. I had seen those parts
before in books and cinemas, that mine
of images whose images were mine
to start with. There was such tender care
in them, with death enough to undermine
all tenderness. I loved that machine of mine.
I loved what it did, befitting a machine.
I had no thought then of the bad machine,
for how could it be bad if it was mine?
It was the machine that was for ever new,
or maybe I could change it, old for new.

And yet it was all new, or almost new
each time. My darlings and desires were mine
to cultivate as I saw fit, as if the new
were all machine and good machines stayed new.
I understood the wearing out of parts
as on another plane, as something new
and still in the future tense. And it was new
to me, the bad machine that tender care
would not maintain, that did not care
for me, bad even then when it was new,
because that is the nature of machine.
There's no machine that's not a bad machine.

My darling look. See, here is a machine,
the bad machine that is our mutual care.
I want you now for all those faulty parts
that over years have learned to move with mine.
Be bad with me, let bad be good as new.

Working Towards the Edge

Finding the edge is the most difficult thing

The spinal column rolled up   fits in the cranial box.
The edges of vision folded   meet at the point of a pin.
The sea in the skull divides,   forming two hemispheres.
The names of those we remember   are listed in two colons.
Order must be maintained   though hardly worth two pins.
Good things must come in twos,   the third becomes an edge.

The skull is always moving   towards an inner edge.
The sea remains in place   affixed with cranial pins.
The mind may be rolled up   and stowed inside the colon.
There must be at least two edges   to divide the hemispheres.
We need two skulls to see   with proper double vision.
We think outside the box   but still within the spine.

The round peg always seeks   the squarest hole for comfort.
The names are safely lodged   at the edges of the sea.
Under the skull the colon   runs right down the spine.
Good edges come in threes   but one will often do.
We work towards the pins   hidden inside the box.
Vision is just the edge   of the nearest cranium.

The spinal column rolled up   is at the edge of reason.
The syntax of the colon   produces hemispheres.
The pins have come to rest   at the edge of the cranium.
Verbs are edgy thoughts: a noun is a poor pin.
The third pin is at the edge: a skull inside a box.
We work towards the sea   that runs right down the spine.

The edge of the spine contains   the names of those we remember.

Leading A Charred Life: Seven Short Songs

John Latham, Observer IV, 1960

1

I had thought to have been charmed
Not framed:
Had thought to be disarmed
Not blamed.

But life hangs fire as if suspended
As if it had been slyly ended.

2

We cannot altogether escape the fact.
The facts are something that can't be quite escaped.
But something is wrong in both thought and act:
The act is thought, and act and thought are shaped.

3

Had I behaved better than I did...
Had sky been lighter, detail more compact...
Had escape ever been possible...
Had I but thought, were it still feasible to act...

4

Someone is raising a hand at a bus stop.
Someone is waving to someone on the other side.
We watch the smile light briefly on a face.
We watch our loved ones make their way through space,
Then space rolling in like a tide,
Entering a bus, a house, a shop.

5

Sometimes the beauty of wood is overwhelming.
We love that which seems warm yet indifferent.
So things burn down, so wood turns to coal,
So coal begins where trees are rife.
So we survive. We lead a (haha) charred life.

6

There is the terrible vehicle of darkness
That runs over us in hope.
There is my hand, there are your fingers.
We hang by our fingertips. We cope.

7

If poetry were just a matter of the air
Playing around the heart
We'd feel a powerful gust beneath our lungs
And call it art –
And art would do, or be, at least, a start.

Limit Frame

after Helen Rousseau

Nothing is limited, there is only a frame
that is endless and not without character,
such as chequers or diapers or neat folds
and knife creases, such as one finds
on a tablecloth or a pair of pressed trousers,
say, on a gentleman of advancing years
whose last recourse is elegance, because
nothing remains, and nothing is limited.

And, say, you took graph paper, and limited
yourself to forty-five or ninety degrees because
there must, after all, be a rule to govern the years
that remain, and you hitch up your trousers
in a businesslike fashion that nobody finds
peculiar, you discover that everything folds
back on itself, even your undoubted character
which is seeking its own unlimited frame.

So there you stand in your unlimited frame
that nonetheless frames you, with a character
others perceive as character, though the folds
of the skin deepen into a condition one finds
intolerable, tucked into dogtooth-check trousers
of which this ribbon is earnest, and so the years
pile up, folded over like skin, limited because,
something must, at the last count, be limited,

because only the frame can ever be unlimited,
so one, meaning you, is still framed, because
the limit is in you not in the frame, and years
resolve down to this, to years of old trousers,
to several millennia of archaeological finds,
to knife-blades, knife-marks, elegance and knife-folds,
a timescale utterly beyond framing or character
where the only character permitted is that of the frame.

Cloudscape

after Helen Rousseau

Look, there are clouds – or is it waves? –
pulsing through a medium, beneath plain paper
and air, something billowing, and, breathe in,
or breathe out, they are still there, those clouds –
or are they waves? – like a gentle washing away
or washing within, such as you feel on the road
in summer when walking down towards the lake
in your head where the grass pulses like water,

and you think of the paper rising through water
within its own frame, the pulp and the lake
and a sieving out, an opening of the road
onto whiteness, that takes you back or further away
into the distance, jostling with the clouds
that are forever inventing images lodged in
vapour and mind, or just on a piece of paper
where even faint shadows resolve into waves,

and here there is nothing but paper unfolding like waves
blown by the air that moves through all paper
that is something you draw on but also draw *in*,
just as the mind will constantly picture in clouds
a face, a body or land that is further away
that it can imagine, in which the limits of road
meet at infinity or at the nearest unruffled lake,
though there is no such thing as wholly unruffled water,

no character, no years, nothing, only the water
that billows through paper as if it were a lake,
as if elegance was water pretending to be road,
a road on which there is no walking away
only *towards* the thing on the paper that is like clouds
that cannot be framed because they're what we're framed in,
and so depicted, as things are depicted on paper,
steadily mounting like all-but-invisible waves.

MINIMENTA
Postcards to Anselm Kiefer

3 Allotments
i.m. Michael Murphy

When I glimpse from the train a clutch
of allotments, a tight row of cabbages or spuds
or garden peas, I think there are gods
beyond gods who live in the bones
of men and women, shivering at their touch;
that when rain falls it weeps hailstones;

that when Bill Evans lays his fingers down
on the keys it is death he is playing
in his own and the world's ear,
in the time allotted, in the proper undertone of fear,
in each cloud that arrives with its gown
of rain, in the moment that bears no delaying;

that the apparatus of 'the Perspex bus-stop
reclaimed' for a hothouse is a new Jerusalem
that is much like the old one; that each raindrop
is a lifetime of damage and new life
at once as it hangs on to the bent leaf
like a lunatic in Hogarth's Bedlam;

that these are the small ordinary days
we all know and live in, huddled inside
the big ones, inside a cosmos we cannot quite
inhabit; that we fall like rain every night;
that it is the gods who are pleased to provide
our allotments, here where one man lays

out a row of something 'implicit
in what it's not'; that the 'twin-tub bleeding rust'
and those prams with missing wheels, those tacit
admissions, may   still be   useful, still
full of purpose, still in possession of a certain will
to serve and not just rot and gather dust.

What we learn once – that life being ordinary
is the extraordinary thing – sticks with us
like clods of soil trapped in the treads of our shoes.
It is the plastic bags and shopping baskets we carry
to and fro, those bags of manure, compost and refuse,
the well-worn crust of the mysterious

that wastes itself and comes round again. I think
of Bill Evans's head bent right down, staring,
it seems, at his feet not the keys. The soft, lost
spaces between head and foot, the loss-bearing,
the unsharing shared, the forgetting of cost
as space opens up just where we stand, on the brink

of music or earth, the universe of barren rock
where everything bears fruit and nothing does,
where the tune moves deeper, an inflorescence
in unresolved chords, with long lines of dock
and nettle and the faint occasional buzz
of the fly hanging on the air, its brief dark presence

zipping off somewhere by itself, into itself.
These small constructions, our scruffy Edens,
those paradise gardens inhabited by gods
much like ourselves: the books on the shelf,
the unrolling of music, the curious odds and sods
of a universe that demand our credence,

they hold us for as long as anything holds.
It is time to go. It is time to pack away
the equipment we are used to: trowel and spade,
and to turn off the music that still unfolds
and won't stop unfolding. We cannot stay,
not here, not anywhere we might have stayed.

The Covering

Between two panes of glass the signs of neglect:
a piece of fuzz, lint, or down that trembles in the draught
of the vent, like a tiny unsustainable craft
on an ocean it cannot solve or perfect.

Now that the wind is up everything beyond
is in a frazzle. The clothes on the line, frail
twigs, the clouds, the whole world setting sail
to an unknown continent over a galactic pond.

Mind too hovers. This is the last day of days,
the crackpots declare, as if days were other than last,
as if we could carry on for ever, not hovering.

As for the fuzz, lint, or down, it holds fast
to the glass either side while the draught plays
across it, as if air were sea, the glass a covering.

Canzone: Terror of, Desire for

Terror of death. Desire for it. Nothing new
in the options *either / or*. No need to dread
the grim reaper, or to worry about the new
morning that won't be there waiting. The new
morning is no morning. There will be other hands
moving through light for whom it remains new
but not for your hands. The moment that is new
each moment, the original first morning,
the unmourned-for, celebrated morning
in which the whole world was, for someone, new
is just another moment or morning, just
a word in a world that never will seem just.

Terror of death. The panic in eyes just
opened, the just registering of the new
imminent possibility that arrives just
when you're rising, alternatively just
as you're going to sleep. You start to dread
the first light, the dawning, the brief unjust
reminder that you're here but only just,
only just seeing the light, the shape of your hands
against the window, the sense of your hands
at your wrists' end as an object, the just-
drawn curtains that frame them and the morning
that draws up like a taxi waiting for the morning.

Desire for death as in 'Not another morning
after such a night with yet another pillow to adjust
before we can get on with life.' Not morning
if the chair is fixed, the bed fixed, the morning
fixed with its catheter and bag, the bag new,
new as the nurse. How to survive the morning
in twilight, answering to 'How do we feel this morning?'
Desire for the death that is an object of dread
and desire, desire itself being the object of dread...
and so you survive more windows, taxis, mornings.
You listen to the traffic breathing. Your hands
lie there before you, but can you move those hands?

You, meaning *me*, meaning *us*, that forest of hands
sticking from sleeves, today and every morning:
it is the *you/me* I'm watching. I touch your hands,
yours touched by mine, which are our mutual hands,
but when I withdraw mine, your hands are just
themselves, while mine are gloves covering hands,
gloves I take off now to expose your hands.
It is as if the whole world were made new,
the terror, the desire, experienced as new.
The morning takes us both in its warm hands
then suddenly drops us in its own moment of dread
as if it could be surprised or shocked by dread.

But let us have no truck with any dread
as sudden as this. Let's consider our hands
as objects of astonishment, the dread
suspended as if for ever, not so much dread
as desire for astonishment and morning,
desire with an aspect that we might call dread,
(but can we have the desire without the dread?)
And so we'd argue on seeking the just
argument, the proper balance that is only just
a balance, more exhilaration than dread,
affirming that the case is always new
because we are ourselves always as new?

So, being old, must always strikes us as new.
So there's the balance that we know is just.
So there is always time and always morning.
So there's the taxi waiting, there my hands,
both yours and mine, to measure out the dread.

Long view

Sometimes light wants to clutch whatever it can:
trees, hedges, spires, an ordinary roof,
until the tops of things vanish completely
into a sky wholly shadow-proof.

It's like a subtle, almost silent burning, the fire
cold and buoyant, tipping skyward.
Long views, long frozen clarities: unreal
distances, half-moon above high wood,

and everything light, weightless, unborn.
Rooks labour past, ice darkens a little
as if by contrast, mud cracks underfoot,
our own bodies ablaze, refusing to settle.

From the Armchair

It was green, it was silent, the rain fell
Without any noise whatsoever and the bed
Lay unmade in the tall room
Where nothing moved throughout the afternoon.
It was late, later than ever, in the time
Before time began. The room was melancholy,
Grown deaf to itself. It was round about four now.
In other rooms chairs and tables
Held their usual conference. All day
It had been raining, and through the window
Fields stretched and gathered themselves for evening.

And then he spoke as if from the armchair,
His voice rising a little before him.
There was a kind of grating sound in him
Which was the sound of rain or furniture.
And then more rain, and then the evening falling.

My Father's Eyes in Old Age

Eyes may be windows and, look!
his have been left flapping open.

Through the window a room
of which there is only the evidence
of semi-darkness and guess-work.

I am wary of those eyes
in case they are mine
in case they tell me everything
about the solitary affair
of being who is and am.

One day the room will have to be cleared
of both him and myself, the window be closed
and the curtains drawn,

those curtains always in evidence,
the semi-darkness, the privacy,
the drawing together, the flapping open,

and a voice, faintly audible, like a distant radio
from which I pick up the voices:
my father, my son.

Canzone: Animal

My father sits in the armchair. I watch him blow
out air that fills the room. He's reckoning
how much air remains to him. I too blow
out air, our two breaths rising blow for blow.
I see his hands curled tight. They are animal
claws, old bones. One gust of wind would blow
him away. He couldn't ward off the blow.
He is so grey he almost looks like smoke,
a curling wreath of ancient cigarette smoke,
the kind that in his youth he'd gently blow
in front of him, over a plate of chicken bones,
his fingers now very like chicken bones.

Whatever are we to do with all those bones?
Should we take the dust and gently blow
it into the fire? Dust may settle on bones
but these are living organs, living bones
that must for ever be shifting, reckoning
up their own vertebrae, all those fiddly bones
adding up to a figure, a figure not just bones
but flesh and tissue and blood, pure animal,
whole animal, the spirit that we mean by animal.
Touch the hand, the soft pad round the bones.
Can all this vanish in a puff of smoke?
Show me the mirror. Let me see the smoke.

But maybe that is all we do see – smoke
curling into a face, illusion, phantom bones.
We read shape into everything and smoke
is apt to read shapes into, cloud and smoke:
both incidentals. Put lips together and blow.
You know how to blow? Then blow away the smoke
and see what remains, that *nothing* after *smoke*,
that nothing hardly worth the reckoning,
that, all the same, we must be reckoning.
The shadow moves across him, much as smoke
drifts over landscape where some animal
is grazing quietly, being nothing but animal.

Perhaps he is that grazing animal
we glimpse through fog that may be drifting smoke.
There is in his eyes a trace of animal,
just as there is in mine. What frightened animal
is scampering there on delicate bones
in the distance? Then which is the true animal?
The one that grazes, or scampers? What animal
does both? And that field across which high winds blow
bending the trees? Will the armchair too blow
away? What is it to blow away an animal?
Even animals come to a final reckoning.
Time is not infinite even by animal reckoning.

Words turn round, recur: invite a reckoning.
We sprinkle words like dust. Intelligent animal,
shrinking in the armchair, beyond reckoning
of words, here's what words have to offer: the reckoning
is in language which is itself a blur of smoke,
a mirrored cliché full of blind reckoning.
But what else, dear animal, can reckoning
achieve apart from this structure made of bones
and syntax, accident and echo; brittle bones
of sound, the tongs and bones, the reckoning
of syllable on syllable, the rhythm, blow on blow,
of pace and run, till we come by that final blow.

The chest rises, the lung dilates. Suck and blow!
Keep moving, thoughts; listen out for bones
whispering in the flesh, their song like smoke,
their words those befitting the fleet animal
glimpsed in the distance, leaping into reckoning.

When Night Falls It Will Be Orderly

When night falls it will be orderly
Proceeding at no more than one house at a time.
Beyond the curtains it will envelop the garden,
Laying itself down in courses, like bricks,
To block in the house, to wall it up
In the time it must dream in.

And the time it must dream in
Is only a prelude to the long waking up,
That unbuilds the dark, dismantling the bricks
Of the house to bury them deep in the garden,
Constructing a new house of light, windowed with time,
So that days may follow, perfectly orderly.

*

But sometimes night descends unremittingly,
As if with a purpose, distinct as the pole star
That seems to fix it like a nail in the wall,
And it hangs there for ever, its low edge descending
As if to a call at the bottom of the ocean
That only blind creatures can hear or respond to.

It is what all creatures fear and respond to.
It is the lung tightening, a drop of ice in the ocean,
That moment of night when the dark keeps descending.
It is table, and chair, and cupboard, and door, and the wall.
Only outside, in the infinite distance, the pole star
Hangs and glitters to nail things unremittingly.

MINIMENTA
Postcards to Anselm Kiefer

4 Stones, trees, wind, river

Under the stones in the quarry, something
catches your eye; something
in the schoolyard where wind
fiddles with leaves and dust
which flies up and leaves you blind:
a horde of red leaves, avalanche of rust.

*

The trees are children, huddling together
at the far end of the field. Look, they
are enormous. Let them stay
where they are with their enormity
a good field's length away. Let weather
beat them without malice or pity.

*

Weather will run its fingers through
the railings where we hung our gloves.
Rain will fall on our shoes and lost scarves.
Feet will patter like rain through our fraught nerves.
Let each imagine losing what he or she loves
without recompense and then try to make do.

*

Almost dusk. Almost invisible. Surge
of water under the feet, a dim
grumbling, and then doves scuffle,
above us out of sight, on the verge
of night. Underneath, the slim
line of silver with its discreet ruffle.

*

The spatter the glimmer the clarity,
the sheer insistent untroubled drive
of it, stripping light
down to essentials, its clear delight
in movement, in the cold certainty
of its voice, in being briskly alive.

*

The blackberries are ripening. One black
among five green in the sun. Fields thick
with light. The wind is a soft hand in your back.

It makes everything move. Now days
too have started to shift. It is late
summer, no reason to panic.
Clouds have begin to congregate
on the horizon, delicate veils of grey.

*

Veils and wind. All gentleness.
What's at the bottom it? The eye
that sees, the ear that hears, the cry
in the bones, the slow unfolding
of pain in its torn floral dress.
The smell of winter. A distant scolding.

*

And song, such as this, not song but speech
And yet song. The dove's *hurr* in the eaves.
Monotone. Vibration. The faint screech
at the back of the throat. The rasp of air
against the yellowing leaves.
Nature in its underwear.

Our Beautiful Mothers

(for Henry Layte)

Our beautiful mothers are leaning against a doorway
with windblown hair and a girlish grin.
They are eternal and terrified and slim
with perfect skin.

Our beautiful mothers are clutching towels
on the hotel terrace in their sweet white shoes.
Their friends are tucking their hair up and smiling
with all to lose.

The air is acid and kind and ruthless.
Our beautiful mothers are stuck in 1954,
their hearts hovering, whole and broken,
in the draught, by the door.

A Photograph in Old Age

So light entered the camera, if only for
a fraction of a second which was enough
time for a draught to slip through the door

or a feather to rise in the faint puff
of wind, or the pupils of her eyes to dilate
and the conceiving of one off-the-cuff

remark about time. Even so she could wait
for time to pass, whole years of it, and slow
the moment down to no particular date,

she, being ninety, and smiling, in a flow
of moments, far too many to note or count,
like watching a feather, or hearing the wind blow

without any desire to keep track of the amount.

A Blue Shirt

There are moments that soul exists
as intensely as the blue of a shirt
or the landscape sliding by a train window,
not as an item of belief
but as a figure it might be possible to know,
to greet, embrace, to violate or hurt
in a space between love and grief,
fine as a set of delicate wrists,

and the notion that wrists might be cut occurs
to you as a thought it is natural to think,
as natural as a pen sliding across a page
or the busy look of, say, a woman
as she taps at her keyboard, of no particular age
but still in a position to dream or sink
into the arms of someone
in an unframed future that is undoubtedly hers.

Just so Beethoven picks at the same scabs
time and again as if soul were an itch
as real as the skin in which he squirms,
in a time like the landscape that's gone
in the dark as the train moves, whose terms
are echo and echo, as if soul were a rich
relative you might touch for cash or a loan
to tide you over a few unpaid tabs.

And it may be the soul is coloured blue
like that shirt which is as real as anything
that music might dream of, or the woman
typing might imagine as her fingers
move over the keys till her work is done,
or the vanished landscape that is about to sing
in the dark, while the soul lingers
at the window seeking a frame to look through.

Dead Child

after Pompeo Batoni

The robes, the cloth, the vase, the veil, the bow,
The posy, the leaves, the rising cloud, the lips.
These were ourselves, this is the cloth that slips
into shapes of cowls and hoods we cannot know.
We cannot decode ourselves. We move below
our surfaces, our griefs, our flowers, the tips
of our fingers. We know what it is that grips
the child in her numbed sleep, what winds still blow
about her. We put our ears to the cloud to hear
vibrations of the air, we measure our wrists
for pulse. We mist mirrors, move in our sleep
as if awake, make energies from fear
accumulated in our veins. We have made lists
of the dead. Our metaphors run deep.

Survival

after Michael Andrews

1

Floating is next to drowning
and though the metaphor of dark
is simply metaphor the metaphor is cold.

Look, our children float against the cold
and though we hold them against the dark
we know the sea's own metaphors for drowning.

2

Those tender bubbles, sea-scum, illusion
of air, the clashing rocks that contain
the sea, they are our modes, our metaphors.

We cannot help but live through metaphors.
The bay contains the sea, the clashing rocks contain
our hands and bodies, our floating, our illusion

3

of floating, and our pale skin, pale warmth,
the metaphor of childhood we find ourselves
employing time and again, like love, like hands

that bear up bodies that terminate in hands.
Dear children you become almost ourselves –
the metaphorical sea's notion of warmth.

4

My feet dissolve, my lower half in water.
Her face is strewn with hair, so we are joined
in this brief act, as brief as other acts,

as if water, drowning, floating, dark, were acts,
as if my life could float, steady and joined
to yours in the bay's cold metaphors of water.

Perdita

1

Thou mettest with things dying, said the shepherd,
but I with things new born, and the new born
are strange, not quite of the world, and yet
precise, just so, and of it, though we forget
the shapes of things, the violent way they're torn
from us, as if we were no more than a cupboard
in a corner, forgotten most of the time,
then suddenly burgled by the realm of *things*,
the *thing* we are emerging into air
and light, the seeming freedom of just being there;
then loss of freedom, the dense tangle of strings
that binds us, the twigs painted with birdlime
that prevent us singing but which we must sing
like any voice that rises from anything.

2

The statue moves the way that statues move
in human voices, whether in speech or song,
the air empty then suddenly full of us,
the cry that escapes us, the brief preface
of a book we can't read, however short or long,
because it's still unwritten, at one remove
from anything we know. We are the thing
that's written: the ghost-writer, the ghost
that now and then appears at the very back
of the eye, writing its history of lack
and hope, of which it is fated to make the most,
scraping the birdlime, cutting through the string.
Then suddenly the statue's closed eye opens:
the baby's world becomes whatever happens.

3

Of course she's found! Everything is found,
because we keep finding *things*, and ourselves,
in the *look* of things. The collector, who delves
through boxes of junk, keeps his eye to the ground
and the look of the thing rises like some peculiar
whale, as yet unclassified by zoologists.
World is ocean: there are *things* beyond official lists
at the bottom, sightless things such as we are,
not yet ready to see, like a baby's eye
moving to light as rhythm, pain, intrusion,
revelation. We are found in our confusion.
We are the revelation, the expected reply
of the deep lost bed, in the least likely quarter
of the universe: the king and queen's lost daughter.

Actually, yes

Somewhere between the highly spectacular *No*
and the modest *yes* of the creatures, word
arises and claims its space. *No* can afford
fireworks and a grand entrance, but *yes* must go
barefoot across floorboards. *No* can extend
its franchise over the glossolalia
of the imagination: yes discovers failure
in a preposition impossible to offend.
No demands success and receives reviews
of the utmost luminosity while *yes*
is damned with faint praise. No profits by excess:
yes has little to say and even less to lose.
The full Shakespearean ending is *No* with its raised brow.
Yes disappears off stage and will not take a bow.

Look, here's a very small *yes*. Now watch it run
its almost invisible race through nature. How
does it know where to go? Where is it now?
Right there! Just there! Like a picture of no one
in particular it looks surprised to be seeing
itself approach a selfhood hardly likely. See
it hesitate as it approaches the sheer possibility
of emergence on the very edge of being.
Always off-centre, its marginal affirmation
of life's distant provinces will be rewarded
with the briefest of smiles when smiles can be afforded
while monstrous *No* boldly addresses the nation.
But now and then, the honest citizen will confess,
when asked, to a weakness of sorts, whispering *Yes*.

Well, *yes*. Actually, *yes*.

We Love Life Whenever We Can

for Mimi Khalvati, after Mahmoud Darwish

We love life whenever we can.
We enter the grocer's, the baker's, the chemist's
   the post office daily.
We love life whenever we can.
We borrow each other's books and paperclips
   and forget to return them.
We spruce ourselves up for a meeting, order
   a taxi, climb into a bus or a train.
We love life whenever we can
   and so we sign letters and cards and spend
   the evening walking the street
when the winter is fiercest and the light
   in the windows and amusement arcades
   snarls at the darkness and the sea is quietly chomping at
   the cliff and the owl and the rat and the fox move over and
   through and we hear them and listen.
We love life whenever we can.

Songlines

Timing is all, and as your eyes move along
the page, like a typewriter, pressing the return
key, you begin to hear the riff of time's song-

lines, filling up, taking over. So you turn
round and, there in the mirror, you find a script
written without your permission, which, you learn,

is the script of your life in progress, a life stripped
from you and turned into a pattern that is more
pattern than you'd like, stricter, more tight-lipped

more revealing...
                    ...But then, you ask, how can we restore
the body into its shapes, send the music
of time into reverse? Is there a way to score

music so it holds us in eternity in some classic
frozen moment? Are the shapes we discover behind
our backs capable of movement – jerkily physic-

al, broken, like this line – into ourselves, refined
like oil, or gold? Or, say, a hand, two eyes,
a mouth, each fine detail singing in an unlined

unwritten poetry that takes everyone by surprise,
the street itself moving in time, its music faint
but relentless, of happening, of song-lines as cries.

Mony Mony

When *Mony Mony* starts up the room stops
whatever it's doing and begins to frame
something it needs to say. The music is a game
it learns then forgets. Temperature drops
inside it as if time were running backwards
to where Tommy James falls through a trapdoor
of memory and disappears through floor after floor
till he ends up here with these notes and these words.
The Shondells tremble with electricity. Drums
generate invisible bodies in the dark
holding a grey diffuse space and charging all
of it. *Here she comes now*. Here is the spark
that passes between them. Here are the magical
ingredients: death, fury, yearning. *Here she comes*.

Easy Listening

It was the long melodic lines that held them together,
chords wound about the limbs of the expected.
When they were falling apart it was what protected
their fragile heads from turning into lather.

They wanted passions they recognised in their sleep
because their sleep had never been unbroken.
There were too many mornings they had woken
to ice, fire, exhaustion, filth; to the cheap

Music others referred to, that they themselves held dear,
their clichés priceless and dark as their own lives:
Songs without Words, Für Elise, the long knives
of aspiration sharpening in the ear.

McGuffin's Tune

1

You whistle it cheerily. It is an ordinary morning,
Just as the crop-spraying plane swoops menacingly low
Or the train enters the tunnel, as gathering birds grow
Unpleasantly intrusive, as the desperate warning

Phone call sets you off across an alien landscape.
What is it called? Where's memory when you need
To discover elemental truth? Notes bleed
Through your ear as you are plotting your escape.

And then a statuesque blonde woman with hair
Like a fortress appears at the corner of your eye
And the whole world tips into chaos. Uncertain

Of your role in this, you contemplate an affair
That ends in horror. What is the tune? And why
Whistle it now, just there, by the shower curtain?

2

McGuffin is the empty box on the baggage rack.
McGuffin is the nothing that makes your fortune.
McGuffin is the alternative name for the tune
You are whistling as shadows shift at your back.

McGuffin the name. So terribly pleased to meet you.
But are you the true McGuffin, the real McCoy?
Is McGuffin a man or an ingenious toy
Whose function is to unmask you then beat you?

Whistle the tune and keep on whistling, it is
What everybody does in the dark after all.
The first four bars are simple but the next

Four you've forgotten. You chase them through cities
Of guilt and hurt until you hear them call
Like death itself: clear, serious, perplexed.

The Time It Takes

Quick time. Slow time. Time flies

By the time they got to Phoenix it was late.
Quick went the movie but the talk was slow
Down empty roads with hours to navigate.

From Tucson up through Arizona state
There's nothing you would recognise or know.
By the time they got to Phoenix it was late.

It's like an anecdote you'll not relate.
You watch dust fly as wind begins to blow
Down empty roads with hours to navigate.

Time flies like dust, no time to contemplate
The journey. You go where you have to go.
By the time they got to Phoenix it was late.

The things you say! The words will not run straight
So time moves on with nothing left to show
Down empty roads with hours to navigate.

Let's cut the talk completely, wipe the slate.
They drove in silence and preferred it so.
By the time they got to Phoenix it was late
Down empty roads with hours to navigate.

Cryogenic: The Big Freeze

Everything comes to an end – but that's OK.
Few of us look to *Tithonus* as a model,
nor are we determined to freeze up,
to preserve heads and bodies just so we can
be micro-waved back into life much later.
I don't desire it. Do you? Are you still there?

Everything comes to an end. Nothing there
but ending. So how are you then? OK,
it's just that the ending ought to arrive later
according to an altogether different model.
So let it arrive as and when it can
before the nerves finally freeze up.

But voice too begins to freeze up.
Words come out frozen and simply lie there.
Our words are mere blocks of ice the world can
carve its initials on. I'm freezing but OK.
How about you? *Are words a working model
of the universe?* I'll get back to you later.

Later is how it goes on. *Later* and ever *later*.
The desire prematurely to freeze up
then revive is based on the standard model.
The words return. I can see them right there,
waiting in line. You wait for the OK,
it comes along. The form does what it can

to engage in the usual catch-as-catch-can
of ingenuity and faith. It is only later
we begin to freeze, suddenly not OK.
I'm on the train when the track starts to freeze up.
I'm frozen. Our minds have gone. *Nothing there.*
I've said that before. There is no other model.

Outside: the landscape. Temperate fields. Model
houses. The disasters of war. The old tin can
filling with rain. A man asks: *Touch me there,*
Just below the heart. Let ice come later.
For now: fire, that no power can ever freeze up.
For now: life. For now: everything is OK.

Here is the model. Who knows about later?
Poems do what they can not to freeze up.
It's language that survives. O K spells OK.

If You Say So

If you say this and I say the opposite,
and there are potential areas of agreement,
we might agree to synthesise our views.

If we failed to synthesise our views,
our sharp differences would appear the sharper,
our language more bladed, our edges more abrasive.

If language became bladed, edges abrasive,
our teeth, our nails, like fangs and claws,
might be deployed to defend our positions.

So this is deployment, this is the position,
these serrations that serve for decoration
under normal circumstances, are themselves the issue.

These are the normal circumstances. This is the issue.
We are ourselves, our teeth, nails and serrations.
The red is blood; black, death; the white, surrender.

There is, after all, a moment of surrender.
There is, after all, a phase of blood and death.
These are abstractions on a piece of paper.

It is, after all, only a sheet of paper.
These grand abstractions are too literal
and quite beside the point. That's if you say so.

Say So

If you *say* so, say so. If you *don't* say so, say so.
If you *say* you say so, don't say you *don't* say so.
If you say, *say* so: don't *say* you say, just *say*.
Just say. Just *say* so. Don't say *I* say so, just *say* so.
I just say *this*. I *say* I just say this. So *you* say.
Say it. Say it just *so*. Say it *is* so.
It *is* so if you *say* so.
It *is* so, so *say* so.

A Man Without a Face

There was a man without a face
He could not grasp it
He could not imagine it
He could not see it

He swam through the air faceless
Like a bladed instrument
Like a swatch of cloth
Like stone rolling uphill
Like a cloud seeking itself in a pond
Like a likeness without a mirror
Like a word
Like a shout
Like breath
Like nothing on earth.

Am I nothing on earth, he felt his tongue asking
Am I feather or stone or leaf
Am I all fingers and thumbs
All arms and legs
All bone and no dog
All wind and no chest

He ached in the depth of his eyes
He hurt in the caves of his ears
His heart dragged in him
His liver and kidneys and pancreas
And all his unnumbered organs
Were faceless and unnumbered

What is it to be faceless, God asked
Since Gods are not given to imagining

Here take my face, said God.
There's nothing behind it.
I've faces enough.

Magister

And there he goes strutting, as if he owned all space,
King of Invented Infinities, Magister of Blank.
Nothing exists beyond him, nothing existed before,
His truths underwritten by no bank.

I spell it out in syntax so we may be clear.
Is he still speaking
                    Where? Where I can't hear?

What is that he says?
                    Is the voice breaking?

ACKNOWLEDGEMENTS

Acknowledgements are due to the editors of the following publications in which some of these poems first appeared: *Black Box Manifold*, *Cork Literary Review*, *Free Verse*, *Jerry*, *Kaffe Klatsch*, *London Magazine*, *Mad Hatter's Review*, *Manchester Review*, *Nasty Little Press*, *Ofi*, *Poetry Review*, *The Rialto*, *The Shop*, *The Spectator*, and *1110*.

Many of these poems were a product of a collaboration with artists Caroline Wright, Helen Rousseau and Phyllida Barlow under the title *Respond / Reply*. I am immensely grateful to them and to Arts Council England for opening new doors.

'Actaeon' was commissioned by the the National Gallery and appeared in *Metamorphosis: Titian* (National Gallery, 2012). 'Gypsy Music' was commissioned by BBC Radio 3. 'The Pram in the Hall' was commissioned by BBC Radio 4. 'McGuffin's Tune' appeared in *Split Screen* (Red Squirrel Press, 2012). 'The Covering' was commissioned by and appeared in *Poems of Hope, Courage and Comfort*. 'Meeting Walt' was commissioned by and published in *Jubilee Lines* (Faber and Faber, 2012). 'Working Towards the Edge' appeared in *Adventures in Form* (Penned in the Margins, 2012).